W9-BHI-574

Developed and produced by Ripley Publishing Ltd

This edition published and distributed by:

Mason Crest
450 Parkway Drive, Suite D, Broomall, PA 19008
www.masoncrest.com

Printed and bound in the United States of America

First printing
9 8 7 6 5 4 3 2 1

Ripley's Believe It or Not!
Incredible World
ISBN: 978-1-4222-3151-7 (hardback)
Ripley's Believe It or Not!—Complete 8 Title Series
ISBN: 978-1-4222-3147-0

Cataloging-in-Publication Data on file with the Library of Congress

PUBLISHER'S NOTE
While every effort has been made to verify the accuracy of the entries in this book, the
Publishers cannot be held responsible for any errors contained in the work. They would
be glad to receive any information from readers.

WARNING
Some of the stunts and activities in this book are undertaken by experts and should not
be attempted by anyone without adequate training and supervision.

Ripley's Believe It or Not!

Download The Weird

INCREDIBLE WORLD

www.MasonCrest.com

INCREDIBLE WORLD

Sensational places. Discover a planet that is beyond belief. Be amazed by the man with 94 children, the bizarre Goat Jump Festival in Spain, and the incredible three-year bike journey from Alaska to Argentina.

A competitor takes part in the mud-pit belly flop contest at the Rednack Games in East Dublin, Georgia...

Clever Camouflage

After the catastrophic raid on Pearl Harbor on December 7, 1941, the Army Corps of Engineers raced to hide the Lockheed Burbank Aircraft Plant in California to protect it from a possible aircraft attack. This was no time for half measures—the Corps opted for deception on the grandest scale, covering every inch of the plant with camouflage netting to make it look like a rural subdivision from the air. Aircraft hangers, factory buildings, runways, planes, as well as the accommodation and everyday comings and goings of the 90,000 employees, took cover beneath the netting. On top, to create a countryside illusion, neighborhood scenes were painted on canvas, fake houses and hundreds of imitation shrubs and trees were built, and rubber automobiles were strategically placed. The canopy was even strong enough to support people hired to ride bicycles randomly. To an enemy pilot, the scene would have seemed perfectly authentic. Below cover, the plant's vital wartime role carried on as normal.

Lockheed ▶ manufactured more than 19,000 planes during World War II, many of them "under the net."

▲ Mock trees were created from chicken wire that had been treated with an adhesive. Chicken feathers were then stuck on top to provide a leafy texture.

◀ ▼ Life continued as normal beneath the huge canopy, with workers having space to park their cars and able to hold mass meetings.

HOLLYWOOD GETS INVOLVED

Disney Studios designed the camouflage used at Lockheed, and the detail and techniques used in Lockheed's camouflage bore many similarities to those in nearby Hollywood's film-set construction. Warner Studios were only a couple of miles away from Lockheed and were also disguised during World War II—but were made to look like the Lockheed plant—to deflect a possible hit away from the important airplane-production site!

▼ The only buildings on view were those that looked like typical rural dwellings or farm buildings.

▼ The peaceful, rolling countryside above the plant.

UNCOVERED

HIDDEN

In the Indian state of Meghalaya, ancient tree vines and roots are trained to stretch horizontally across rivers in order to create latticework structures that are solid enough to be used as bridges. Some of these living bridges are 100 ft (30 m) long and can support the weight of 50 people at the same time.

LIVING BRIDGE FACTS

- Conventional wooden bridges would quickly rot in the region, which is one of the wettest places on the planet, receiving around 590 in (1.5 m) of rainfall per year—about 30 times more than London, England.

- The Indian rubber tree—*Ficus elastica*—grows on riverbanks and supports its upward growth by sending out low-level vines, which grip onto boulders, other trees, and soil. Some 500 years ago, villagers began guiding these roots out over rivers, hoping to create river crossings.

- The roots used in the bridges are about 6 in (15 cm) thick.

- It takes about 15 years for a tree bridge to be established, but they can then last for hundreds of years—and, unlike man-made structures, they grow stronger with age.

- The Umsiang Double-Decker Root Bridge in Nongriat is unique for being two root bridges—one stacked over the other.

▣ **BAD SINGING** The Philippines House of Representatives passed a law in October 2010 making it a crime to sing the country's national anthem poorly. A guilty singer could get up to two years in jail.

▣ **PUMPKIN RACE** Each year Ludwigsburg Castle in Germany stages a pumpkin festival, the highlight of which is a giant pumpkin boat race in the former royal palace's massive fountain. The pumpkins can weigh more than 200 lb (90 kg) before their tops are cut off and their flesh scooped out to turn them into paddleboats. The 2010 festival also featured a giant statue of a seahorse made out of pumpkins.

▣ **POPULATION CENTER** Mongolia covers more than 600,000 sq mi (1.5 million sq km)—about four times the size of Germany—but nearly half its citizens live in one city, its capital Ulan Bator.

▣ **SEA OF CORN** In November 2010, a grain silo collapsed in Norwalk, Ohio, spilling more than 100,000 bushels of corn and creating a "sea of corn" 12 ft (3.6 m) deep that knocked a nearby home from its foundation.

▣ **HYDRANT TOSS** Sherrodsville, Ohio, has an annual fire-hydrant tossing contest. Participants hurl heavy 113-lb (51-kg) hydrants distances of over 20 ft (6 m). A women's competition uses lighter 40-lb (18-kg) hydrants.

▣ **GIANT TREE** Since 1981, the Italian town of Gubbio has created an illumination in the shape of the "biggest Christmas tree in the world" on a mountainside above the town. In 2010, the spectacle boasted more than 800 lights, and used nearly 8 mi (13 km) of cables and thousands of plugs to create a tree that stretched over 2,600 ft (795 m) tall.

▣ **DRIFTWOOD MUSEUM** Bandon, Oregon, has a museum dedicated solely to driftwood, displaying weird and natural shapes from gnarled root balls to whole tree trunks.

SUCKLING COW

A young Cambodian boy feeds himself daily by suckling directly from a cow. The boy had watched a calf nurse from its mother and instinctively did the same thing.

SMALL CEMETERY Ocracoke Island, North Carolina, is home to a cemetery owned by Britain that has only four graves. All four souls were washed ashore from a capsized British trawler in 1942.

CAVE SCHOOL Until 2011, a school in a remote mountain community in Guizhou Province, China, had all its classrooms and its playground in a cave. The 186 pupils at the Getu Village Cave Primary School took their lessons in a vast cave the size of an aircraft hangar, surrounded by bats and lizards. The acoustics helped the school to have the best choir in the area.

OLD-STYLE HOLIDAYS Hotel Morava in Tatranska Lomnica, Slovakia, hosts vacations in the style of the former Communist worker holidays—complete with strict 7 a.m. wake-up calls, compulsory morning exercises, and even a re-enactment of a May Day rally.

SIGNPOST FOREST The Signpost Forest, near Watson Lake, Yukon, Canada, displays more than 65,000 city limits signs that have been collected from around the world. The collection was started in 1942 after a homesick G.I., Private Carl K. Lindley, accidentally drove a bulldozer into the original sign that pointed out the distances to various locations along the Alaska Highway. While carrying out repairs following the accident, Private Lindley added a sign pointing to his hometown of Danville, Illinois. Each year up to 4,000 new signs are added by tourists and visitors as they pass through Watson Lake, so that the Signpost Forest now occupies a couple of acres.

TOTEM POLE Over a three-month period, a 40-ft-tall (12.1-m) redwood tree at Confusion Hill, Piercy, California, was carved by chainsaw into a gigantic totem pole. The pole is the largest free-standing redwood chainsaw carving in the world.

HOBBIT HOTEL Fans of *Lord of the Rings* can stay in an underground hobbit hotel in Trout Creek, Montana. Steve Michaels has built the 1,000-sq-ft (93-sq-m) Hobbit House of Montana into a hill and designed it so that it looks just like Middle Earth from the outside, but has modern comforts such as HD Blu-Ray TV and WiFi access on the inside.

BEDROOM SINKHOLE A sinkhole 40 ft (12 m) deep and 2 ft 7 in (80 cm) in diameter suddenly appeared overnight beneath the bed of a woman's home in Guatemala City in July 2011. Guatemala City is prone to sinkholes because it is built on volcanic deposits and experiences abnormally high rainfall.

GIANT FUNGUS A enormous fungus found in China is 33 ft (10 m) long, 2 ft 7 in (80 cm) wide, and 2¼ in (5.5 cm) thick—and it weighs half a ton. It was discovered living under a fallen tree and is estimated to hold 450 million spores.

Fiery Rider

Believe it or not, this rider from Kyrgyzstan set light to his back during a spectacular fiery stunt at the 2011 Lake Son-Kul folk festival in the north of the country.

HIGH RISK

Thousands of feet above the ground, at the top of a sheer drop, with no safety precautions, and working on an area no wider than a dinner table, a worker takes his life in his hands to transport building materials for a wooden plank road on Shifou Mountain in China's Hunan Province.

THE WORLD'S MOST
DANGEROUS JOBS

- **ICE ROAD-TRUCKERS** Driving hundreds of miles at a time, they power 50-ton trucks carrying vital supplies across frozen Arctic lakes, rivers, and seas, knowing that any crack in the ice could be fatal.

- **SULFUR MINER** Workers in East Java, Indonesia, collect sulfur from the floor of the 660-ft-deep (200-m) acid crater lake of the Ijen Volcano. As well as the fear of volcanic eruption, they endure toxic gases and carry up to 220 lb (100 kg) of mined sulfur by hand for several miles down the mountain every day.

- **ALASKAN CRAB FISHERMEN** These men toil in the Bering Sea seven days a week, often in the dark and without breaks. With a death rate of more than 350 per 100,000 (mostly from drowning or hypothermia), the fatality rate is 50 times that of most workers. On average, one Alaskan crab fisherman dies every week.

- **CROCODILE WRESTLERS** At Thailand's Samphran Elephant Ground & Zoo, men put on a show by wrestling crocodiles for an hour, even putting their head between the jaws of some of the zoo's monster crocs.

STANDING STONES The French village of Carnac is home to more than 3,000 standing stones arranged in straight lines over 5,000 years ago by an ancient civilization.

LIGHTNING STRIKE A single lightning bolt at a military base in Hattiesburg, Mississippi, in June 2011 struck an entire troop of cadets, sending no fewer than 77 of them to hospital.

JUNK WINDMILL In 2002, the village of Masitala in Malawi had electricity for the first time when local resident, William Kamkwamba, built a windmill from junk and spare parts to generate power.

DUCT TAPE FESTIVAL Since 2004, the town of Avon, Ohio, has held an annual festival celebrating duct tape, complete with artistic exhibits made from the tape.

ON THE EDGE Groups of up to six people who enjoy living on the edge can pay $175 per person to walk hands-free for 30 minutes around a high, narrow ledge on the outside of the CN Tower in Toronto, Ontario—attached only by a cable. The ledge is just 5 ft (1.5 m) wide, has no guardrail, and is 1,168 ft (356 m) above ground, but offers exhilarating views of the city and Lake Ontario.

TREE CHAPEL

An 800-year-old oak tree in the French village of Allouville-Bellefosse has two chapels in its hollow trunk. They were built in the late 1600s, along with an exterior spiral staircase, after lightning burned through the tree. Each year, on August 15, a religious pilgrimage is made to the Chapel Oak.

GREAT WALL Following in the footsteps of the country's ancient emperors, in January 2011 the wealthy residents of Aodi, Zhejiang Province, China, built a 23-ft-high (7-m) wall around their village for protection. They created the 28-in-thick (70-cm) wall from more than 70,000 adobe bricks. The only entrance to the village is via a huge iron gate.

HOPPING PROCESSION Echternach, Luxembourg, hosts an annual hopping procession. Up to 9,000 men, women, and children—linked by a chain of handkerchiefs—hop through the streets in celebration of a local saint, St. Willibrord.

FOSSIL FIND In February 2011, miner Jay Wright was working 700 ft (210 m) underground at a coalmine in Webster County, Kentucky, when he discovered a 300-million-year-old shark jawbone.

FOUGHT TSUNAMI While most of the 3,500 people on the Japanese island of Oshima ran to the hills on hearing the March 2011 tsunami warning, 64-year-old Susumu Sugawara took his fishing boat out to sea and rode out a succession of 60-ft-high (18-m) waves. When the tsunami abated, his was the only boat from the island that had not been destroyed.

Pig Parade

At the Lechon (roasted) Pig Parade in La Loma, Philippines, shop proprietors dress up roasted pigs to advertise their businesses—in guises including a singer, a racing driver, and even characters from the movie *Matrix Reloaded*.

SHOCKING SHOWER Lightning can strike twice! Twelve-year-old Alice Svensson of Gothenburg, Sweden, was struck by lightning twice as it traveled through water pipes while she showered. Although badly shocked, she was unharmed.

RIG PODS Visitors to Den Haag, the Netherlands, can pay $75 a night to stay in hotel rooms that have been transformed from oil rig survival capsules. One of the bright orange pods has even been given a James Bond theme, with silk sheets on the bed, champagne, and a vodka martini bar.

SACRED BELL A Buddhist temple bell in Liuzhou, China, weighs 120 tons, stands 30 ft (9 m) tall, measures 20 ft (6 m) in diameter at its widest point, and is engraved with 92,306 sacred Chinese characters.

PRIZE CRASH Truck driver David Dopp of Santaquin, Utah, won a $380,000 Lamborghini sports car in a competition in October 2011, but within six hours of driving it away, he crashed it.

MILITARY PAST The MV Liemba, a ferry that runs across Africa's Lake Tanganyika, was originally built in 1913 as a warship for Imperial Germany.

TOY STORY In April 2012, two-year-old Noah Joel pedaled his toy bicycle over 3 mi (4.8 km) across the busy town of Hamelin, Germany, to visit his grandmother in the hospital, while his mother thought he was playing in his room.

BLIND AMBITION Pete Golsby from Suffolk, England, spent nearly five years building a sports car from scratch—even though he is blind and cannot drive it. He put it together using an engine from an old motorbike, piping from a shower, and car parts donated by friends.

DOOR TO HELL The Door to Hell near Darvaza, Turkmenistan, is a crater—200 ft (60 m) in diameter and 65 ft (20 m) deep—that is filled with burning gas. Geologists ignited it more than 35 years ago so that no poisonous gas could escape from the hole, and it has been burning ever since.

ANCIENT INN The Keiunkan Inn in Hayakawa, Yamanashi Prefecture, Japan, has operated continuously for more than 1,300 years. The hotel boasts a hot spring 2,913 ft (888 m) underground that produces 358 gal (1,630 l) of water at a temperature of 126°F (52°C) every minute.

WORM SHOWER Students at a school in Galashiels, Scotland, ran for cover in March 2011 when dozens of worms suddenly fell from a cloudless sky.

TOXIC TREE The milky white sap of the manchineel tree, native to Florida, the Caribbean, and Central America, is so toxic that just standing underneath it during a rainstorm can cause skin and eye irritation. Burning the tree may cause temporary blindness if the smoke reaches the eyes.

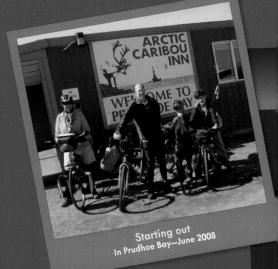

Starting out
In Prudhoe Bay—June 2008

HUGE HAILSTONES More than 20 people were injured when hailstones the size of chicken's eggs hit the Siberian city of Mezhdurechensk on August 14, 2012.

SNAKE VILLAGE Just over 25 years ago, the 160 families in China's Zisiqiao village farmed the land and raised livestock—now they breed more than three million snakes every year for food and use in traditional medicine. The "snake village" was started by a single local farmer, who began by catching wild snakes to sell, and then bred them at home. His practices soon caught on and farming snakes has since brought millions of dollars to what was once a poor village.

GLASS BEACH

The Glass Beach is a beach in Fort Bragg, California, that is completely covered with stone-sized pieces of natural glass in different colors. The beach was used as a public dump during the 1950s and 1960s, which included a lot of glass that ended up in the ocean. The glass has since been deposited back on the beach over a number of years, after the harsh waves and cold waters of the North Pacific Ocean have softened and polished the pieces.

American Odyssey

For nearly three years from June 2008 to March 2011, John and Nancy Vogel and their twin sons Daryl and Davy of Boise, Idaho, cycled the entire length of the Pan-American Highway from Alaska to the tip of Tierra del Fuego, Argentina—a pedaling distance of 17,300 mi (27,850 km). The boys were just ten years old when they set off, making them the youngest people to cycle the length of the Americas.

Ripley's ask

Ripley's spoke to Nancy about her incredible journey.

What inspired you to start this trip with your family? We wanted time together as a family before the kids grew up and flew the coop. As for the route, it could easily have been Asia or Africa or Europe—although there was a special draw to the longest road in the world.

How many miles did you have to cycle each day? Our overall average was a mere 17 miles per day. Although we did cycle 17 miles many days, there were many days when we cycled more and many days we took off completely. We aimed for around 30–50 miles on the days we cycled, but that varied tremendously due to hills, winds, or availability of resources.

What was the hardest stretch of your trip? Northern Argentina. When we crossed into Argentina, our brains told us we were nearly done—our last country means nearly there, right? But Argentina is a HUGE country! We had been warned many times about the winds in Patagonia in southern Argentina, but nobody mentioned the headwinds in the north—and they were horrible! So, mentally we thought we should be nearly there and we had daily unexpected headwinds. That's a very tough combination to cope with!

What was the most rewarding? Arriving in Ushuaia at the end of the world. After spending three years cycling 17,300 miles through 15 countries, to pull up to that sign in Ushuaia announcing that we were at the end of the world was a moment I will never forget. We did it!

Southern Bolivia
("Our planned route through Bolivia was thwarted when a major strike closed one of the cities we would need to pass through. We ended up taking a 400-mile detour up and over the Andes." (August 2010)

In the Colombian Andes
"The Andes took us by surprise with their long, steep climbs. This photo was taken near the top of our first major climb—it was 'only' a 6,000-ft (1,800-m) climb, which, later, would be considered easy. Our longest climb was a whopping 14,856 ft (4,528 m) from sea level to the top of the pass in just 225 mi (362 km)." (August, 2009)

Small town in South America
"Most of our time was spent either out on the open road or in small villages. Large cities were few and far between." (September 2010)

Endless roads
"In Argentina, I never thought we would reach the end of the road!" (November 2010)

Arriving at the end of the world
Ushuaia, Argentina. (March 2011)

CASTLE CLIMB

Ma Jei climbed the 70-ft-high (21-m) wall of Zhonghua Gate Castle, China—without a rope or safety equipment—just so that she could avoid paying the $3.75 admission fee. When other visitors tried to follow her example, two fell and broke their legs, and three others had to be rescued.

CARDBOARD BOATS The Cardboard Boat Museum in New Richmond, Ohio, displays some of the weird and wonderful craft that have competed in 20 years of the annual cardboard boat race on the Ohio River.

SOMALI SPLIT When Somalia's dictator, Siad Barre, was overthrown in 1991, the northwestern part of the country seceded and declared independence as Somaliland. They have a currency, a police force, and democratic elections but are not recognized by any other country.

SIESTA TIME Spain's first National Siesta Championship took place in Madrid in 2010 to help revive the tradition of taking a short sleep after lunch. Competitors were monitored as they tried to doze for 20 minutes on sofas in the middle of a shopping mall. The highest points were awarded to people who managed to sleep for the full 20 minutes, but marks were also awarded for inventive sleeping positions, distinctive outfits, and the loudest snore.

CHINA CENSUS China, the world's most populated country, employed six million people—more than the entire population of Denmark—simply to administer its 2010 population census.

FIRST SNOW In August 2011, a cold blast from the Antarctic brought snow to Auckland, New Zealand, for the first time in 35 years—snow was last seen there in the 1970s. The unusual weather created such excitement that people rushed to post pictures and videos online of the snow as it fell in the city.

UNDERWATER SUITE To celebrate its fifth anniversary, the Conrad Maldives Rangali Island Hotel converted its famous underwater restaurant into a honeymoon suite beneath the waves, complete with a double bed, complimentary champagne breakfast, and uninterrupted views of exotic sea life.

FINGER OF FATE

This cloud in the shape of an arm and a hand was photographed pointing from the sky over Tenerife, Canary Islands, by a British couple on holiday there in October 2011.

Bull Plunge

At the annual *Bous a la Mar* (Bulls-to-the-Sea) festival in Denia, Spain, young bulls run down a street to the harbor chasing revelers who jump into the sea, hotly pursued by the bulls, which are then brought back to land by boat.

SANTA PENTATHLON The 54th World Santa Claus Congress, held near Denmark's capital, Copenhagen, in 2011, featured a Santa pentathlon—a five-discipline event between two teams of Santas, one from Denmark and one from the rest of the world, including the United States, Sweden, Russia, and Germany. The fitness contest required the Santas to throw gifts, fire cannonballs, ride bumper cars, race over an obstacle course, and compete in a horse-race game.

MYSTERY FIREBALL When Croatians spotted a mysterious ball of fire dart through the sky over Bjelovar in February 2011, many thought it was a comet or even an alien attack. Instead, it turned out to be nothing more than a patch of burning grass caught by the wind. Local farmer Marin Kiselic had decided that, with no time to mow his fields, it was cheaper to set them on fire.

TEARFUL BRIDES The Tujia people in Central China maintain an ancient tradition of "crying marriages." Brides begin daily crying a month before the wedding, with female friends eventually joining in so that they can weep together.

UNDERSEA VOLCANOES A chain of 12 huge, underwater volcanoes has been discovered in the icy waters of the Southern Ocean. The volcanoes—some of which are active—are dotted over an area the size of Britain and several are around 2 mi (3 km) high, making them nearly four times higher than the world's tallest building, Dubai's Burj Khalifa.

FAIRY ROCK A builder was forced to redesign a luxury housing estate in Perthshire, Scotland, around a rock because local people said fairies lived under it and would be upset if it were moved.

GLOWING LAKES Gippsland Lakes in Victoria, Australia, glow in the dark—owing to a combination of fires, floods, and algae. The fires of 2006 were followed by severe floods, which washed ash and nitrogen-rich soil into the lakes. When temperatures warmed up in the summer, blue-green algae feeding on the high level of nutrients, appeared across great areas of the water. When the organisms were disturbed, they created a chemical reaction called bioluminescence, which emitted an eerie blue light, making the lake glow at night.

$10 MILLION TREE For Christmas 2010, the Emirates Palace Hotel in Abu Dhabi displayed a jewel-encrusted Christmas tree worth more than $10 million. The tree's branches were draped in bracelets, necklaces, and watches containing diamonds, pearls, emeralds, sapphires, and other precious stones.

The 100-room mansion where the family all live

A giant communal bedroom

THERE ARE 181 MEMBERS OF ZIONA CHANA'S FAMILY (AND COUNTING)

HE ONCE MARRIED TEN WOMEN IN ONE YEAR

HE LIVES WITH THEM ALL IN A 100-ROOM MANSION

A ROTATION SYSTEM OPERATES SO THAT HIS WIVES TAKE TURNS SHARING HIS BED

HE HAS UP TO EIGHT WIVES WITH HIM ALL THE TIME TO WAIT ON HIS EVERY NEED

A TYPICAL DINNER REQUIRES COOKING 30 WHOLE CHICKENS, PEELING 132 LB
(60 KG) OF POTATOES, AND BOILING 220 LB (100 KG) OF RICE

Ziona Chana, 67, is head of the world's largest family—consisting of 39 wives, 94 children, 33 grandchildren, and 14 daughters-in-law. They all live in a rambling four-story house in a hill village in the Indian state of Mizoram, where Ziona is head of a religious sect that allows members to take as many wives as they want. While he has his own double bed, his wives sleep in giant communal dormitories, the youngest women sleeping closest to his bedroom. His oldest wife, Zathiangi, organizes the other wives to carry out the daily household chores so that the compound is run with military precision. The house even has its own school, as well as a vegetable garden big enough to feed the entire extended family.

FULL HOUSE

Eaten great tit!

WICKED PLANTS

Around 70,000 people are poisoned annually by plants in the United States alone. Here are some of the chief culprits.

THE PLANT THAT ALMOST KILLED CLEOPATRA
Strychnine tree *Nux vomica*

Before committing suicide with a poisonous asp, Egyptian ruler Cleopatra was intending to kill herself by ingesting parts of the strychnine tree. However, when she saw that the plant caused her servant to suffer terrible seizures, stiffness, and convulsions, all while conscious, she chose the snake instead.

THE PLANT THAT KILLED LINCOLN'S MOTHER
White snakeroot *Ageratina altissima*

Abraham Lincoln's mother, Nancy Hanks Lincoln, died of deadly milk sickness in 1818 after drinking milk from a cow that had been eating white snakeroot. Every part of the plant contains tremetol, a lethal liquor that causes tremors in livestock before killing them.

THE PLANT THAT CAN STRIKE YOU DUMB IN THE OFFICE
Dumb cane *Dieffenbachia amoena*

A popular office and house plant because it is tolerant of shade, the plant's leaves contain a toxic sap which, if chewed, can cause drooling, swelling, and, in extreme cases, paralysis of the vocal cords.

THE PLANT THAT WAS USED TO EXECUTE SOCRATES
Hemlock *Conium maculatum*

A highly poisonous member of the carrot family, hemlock contains a neurotoxin that results in death owing to lack of oxygen to the heart and brain. Eating just a few leaves can be fatal. The ancient Greek philosopher Socrates was sentenced to death in 399 BC by drinking a mixture containing hemlock.

THE FUNGUS THAT MAKES YOU CRY
Sweater mushroom *Clitocybe dealbata*

Toxins in the sweater mushroom of Europe and North America make you sweat profusely, drool, and cry uncontrollably. These symptoms are followed by blurred vision, vomiting, diarrhea, and painful abdominal cramps.

THE PLANT THAT PARALYZES
Coyotillo *Karwinskia humboldtiana*

A flowering shrub in the buckthorn family and native to Texas and Mexico, the berries of the coyotillo contain deadly neurotoxins that cause a slow but deadly paralysis in both livestock and children.

THE PLANT THAT HOUSES A LETHAL WEAPON
Castor oil plant *Ricinus communis*

Although castor oil has been a medicine for centuries, its seeds contain ricin, a poison that has been used by the Soviet KGB to murder dissidents. It has also been considered for use in chemical warfare. Just one milligram is enough to kill an adult.

KILLER PLANT

A carnivorous pitcher plant at a garden nursery in Somerset, England, killed and ate a great tit—only the second documented case in the world of a pitcher plant eating a bird. The plant's inner wall secretes a nectarlike substance to attract insects, and the bird probably leaned in too far in to catch a bug and became trapped by the plant's slippery, waxy surface. It then fell into the pool of enzymes and acid that is housed at the base of the pitcher. Large pitcher plants often eat rats and frogs, and can completely devour a piece of meat in just a few days.

PLANT LIFE The South Atlantic's arid and volcanic Ascension Island received its diverse plant species in the 1850s when the British Royal Navy populated it with annual shipments of plants from around the world.

DOOMSDAY VAULT Millions of seeds taken from more than 500,000 different crop varieties are stored in a special vault situated 425 ft (130 m) inside a frozen mountain on a remote Norwegian island near the Arctic Ocean. The location for the Doomsday Vault, as it is known, was chosen because it is thought to be about the safest place on the planet to protect the world's seed collections from nuclear war or other disasters.

ORANGE GOO A strange, sticky, orange goo made up from millions of rust fungal spores washed ashore near Kivalina, Alaska, in 2011.

SKELETON VIEW A five-bedroom house in Visby on the Swedish island of Gotland has a medieval tomb and skeleton in the cellar. The house was built in 1750 on the foundations of a Russian church. The kitchen rests on the presbytery, and the tomb containing the skeleton of a Russian man who died about 800 years ago is visible through a glass panel.

WILD ORCHID A single Lady's Slipper orchid growing on the Silverdale Golf Course in Carnforth, Lancashire, England, is the last of its kind growing wild in all of Britain and is protected by police patrols. The orchid, which is more than 100 years old, attracts hundreds of visitors each year, with people traveling over 200 mi (320 km) just to see it.

LONG STREET A single street in central Brazil stretches for 311 mi (501 km). Lined with houses for the whole length, it is almost the equivalent to a street running all the way from San Francisco to Los Angeles.

WATERPROOF VAULT The Crypt of Civilization—a waterproof vault beneath Oglethorpe University in Atlanta, Georgia—was sealed in 1940 and contains objects and information of the day. Its stainless steel receptacles are filled with inert gases and so are designed to last 6,000 years.

TWIN TOWN About 1.5 percent of all human births are twins—but they are over three times more common in the town of Igbo-Ora, Nigeria. The reason for the high level of multiple births is a mystery, but some doctors believe it could be linked to the large amount of the tuberous vegetable yam eaten by the local people.

LONG AND WINDING ROAD

Drivers compete on the twisty 24 Crankle Stilwell Road (also known as the Burma Road) during a hill-climb rally in Guizhou Province, China. The road is 717 mi (1,154 km) long and runs from Yunnan Province, China, to Burma. Over 2,300 laborers lost their lives while building the Chinese section of the road in 1938.

R FLYING HIGH The city of Calipatria, California, sits at an altitude of negative 184 ft (56 m), but its flagpole is just high enough for the U.S. flag to fly right at sea level.

R HOLY STALAGMITE India's ice "Shiva Lingam," a stalagmite that is worshiped by Hindus, was melting in August 2011 because of warmer weather and a record number of vistors generating too much body heat. Over a 40-day period that summer, 620,000 people went to see the holy stalagmite at Amarnath caves in Kashmir.

R CONNECTICUT CORNER If you travel directly north, south, east, or west from the city of Stamford, Connecticut, you will enter the state of New York.

R DRIVE-THRU MORTUARY There is a drive-thru mortuary in Compton, California. The Robert L. Adams Mortuary has a drive-thru viewing option where mourners can see the open casket of a dead relative displayed behind a long bulletproof glass window without getting out of their car.

R COLOSSAL CAVE At more than 650 ft (198 m) high and almost 500 ft (152 m) wide, Hang Song Doong, a cave in Vietnam, is large enough to contain several 40-story buildings.

Buddhist Body

Inside a large pot at a temple in Fujian Province, China, construction workers found the body of a Buddhist nun that had been buried for 32 years. Although Chen Zhu's corpse had not been embalmed, it was so well preserved that it has now been wrapped in gauze and coated in black lacquer and gold foil to make a human body statue. Buddhists say the nun's vegetarian diet kept her body in a good state.

VOODOO SUPERSTITIONS

- If a woman visits you first thing on a Monday morning, it is bad luck for the rest of the week.
- If you shake a tablecloth outside after dark, someone in your family will die.
- To keep her husband faithful, a woman should add a little of her blood to his coffee.
- Laying a broom across the doorway at night keeps witches at bay.
- To stop a widow remarrying, cut all of her husband's shoes into small pieces as soon as he is dead.
- Borrowing or lending salt is bad luck.
- Turning someone's picture upside down automatically gives them a headache.

Voodoo is a traditional religion from West Africa. It is based on a belief that animals and inanimate objects, known as fetishes, have spiritual powers. These fetishes are used in voodoo rituals. Powders made from various animal parts are administered by voodoo priests, or *bokors*, which can seemingly send people into a trance. Traditional West African voodoo was transported to Haiti in the Caribbean and to the southern United States, particularly Louisiana, where it mixed with Catholicism. Voodoo mixes have been linked to reports of real-life "zombies" in Haiti, with victims supposedly stuck in a trance for years.

Voodoo healers claim to be able to cure a vast range of sicknesses by slicing open human flesh and inserting into the wound a black powder made from the body parts of dead animals. Akodessewa Fetish Market in Togo, West Africa, is a voodoo supermarket—an outdoor pharmacy where thousands of animal body parts, including crocodile heads, monkey testicles, snake skin, and elephants' feet, take the place of conventional medicine. People from all over the region descend on the market—the biggest of its kind in the world—to buy fetishes, to cure family illnesses, or simply to enhance any of their particular abilities.

To concoct these magic charms, voodoo priests grind up the animal parts with herbs and burn the mixture on a fire to create a black powder. Three incisions are made in the patient's back or chest into which the powder is then rubbed. During this ritual the priests often work themselves into and out of trances, as if possessed by spirits.

The different animal body parts are said to correspond with the human body. So the hand of a dead chimpanzee might be ground down and inserted into the flesh of a soccer goalkeeper to help with his agility, while marathon runners are given powder made from the head, heart, and legs of a horse to increase their speed. Powdered monkey testicles are sometimes used to help women conceive.

The market also sells animal-bone statues to ward off evil spirits and protect homes.

The heads of dead leopards are used by voodoo priests to make a powdered medicine to cure human head and brain conditions.

VOO

DOO

A voodoo witch doctor, known as "King Fox," poses in a ceremonial animal hide costume in Africa.

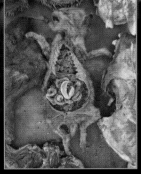

Cats with their stomach ripped open line the market stalls at Lomé, Togo. The stench from the market is described as foul.

In Haiti, voodoo dolls, or fetishes, can be seen in graveyards. Some believe they act as messengers to the spirit world, and to help contact loved ones. This doll, found in the national cemetery in Port-au-Prince, belongs to a voodoo priest who practices in the graveyard.

Visitors to Akodessewa Fetish Market can buy all manner of medicinal skulls, including crocodile heads, vultures, owls, dogs, turtles, rodents, and mummified bats.

A voodoo priest caked in mud in Port-au-Prince, Haiti, in November 2011. Haitian voodoo believers bathe in sacred mud pools and sacrifice animals as part of an annual voodoo festival in Plaine du Nord, in the north of the country.

Voodoo medicine is so powerful that voodoo priests, or *bokors*, are believed to have used it to create real-life "zombies." Clairvius Narcisse was declared dead by doctors in Haiti and buried in 1962, only to reappear 18 years later, claiming that he had been poisoned through a skin abrasion by a *bokor* and then brought back to life. He said that soon after his "death" he had been revived by the *bokor*, drugged with plant toxins that impaired his brain function, and put to work as a zombie slave on a plantation. When the poison administered by the voodoo priest was analyzed, it was found to contain puffer fish, one of the world's most toxic creatures. The toxin causes paralysis and a strange coma in which patients claim to retain consciousness despite being unable to move. That was how Clairvius came to be buried alive. When he did eventually reappear, he bore a scar on his cheek that he said was caused by one of the nails in his temporary coffin.

UNDERSEA RIVER Differences in temperature and salt content cause water from the Mediterranean to flow into the Black Sea as an underwater river, complete with waterfalls and a riverbed on the sea floor.

TORNADO RECORD On April 27, 2011, a record-breaking 312 tornadoes were recorded over the United States' southern States in a 24-hour period starting at 8 a.m.—more than double the previous record of 148 twisters in a single day in 1974. Four of the April 2011 tornadoes achieved the most powerful ranking possible—EF5 on the Enhanced Fujita Scale—whereas normally such destructive twisters are recorded only once a year or less.

WORLD SIGN A signpost in Lynchville, Maine, points to Norway (14 mi/22 km), Paris (15 mi/24 km), Denmark (23 mi/37 km), Naples (23 mi/37 km), Sweden (25 mi/40 km), Poland (27 mi/43 km), Mexico (37 mi/60 km), Peru (46 mi/74 km), and China (94 mi/151 km). The towns are all in Maine and the distances from Lynchville are genuine.

TSAR BELL The bronze Tsar Bell, which sits in the grounds of the Kremlin, Moscow, Russia, weighs over 200 tons, stands more than 200 ft (6 m) high, has a diameter of 21 ft 8 in (6.6 m), and is 2 ft (60 cm) thick. Cast in 1735, the bell—the biggest in the world—was damaged two years later by fire, the heat from which caused a 12-ton piece to shatter. The bell has been used as a chapel, with people entering and exiting via the broken area.

CROOKED FOREST

The town of New Czarnowo, Poland, is home to a bizarre forest near the Odra River, where hundreds of pine trees display large bends in the bottom of their trunk, before growing vertically as normal. Surrounding trees are completely straight. The reason behind their deformity is a mystery, and explanations range from man-made techniques used to shape the wood for use in furniture or boats, to extreme environmental conditions when the trees were young.

TREE HOME After graduating from college and with his parents moving to Hawaii, Corbin Dunn built a tree house and lived in it for five years. Located 40 ft (12 m) above ground at the back of the family home in Santa Cruz, California, the tree house had electricity and boasted a fully functional shower and toilet.

NEW ISLANDS New islands regularly appear and disappear off the coast of Pakistan near the Makran Desert over a matter of months. They are created by volcanoes of mud that erupt from deep within the Earth.

LONGEST CONSTITUTION With 444 articles, 12 schedules, and 94 amendments totaling more than 117,000 words, India's Constitution is the longest written constitution of any independent country. By contrast, the U.S. Constitution is the shortest, with just seven articles and 27 amendments, giving a total of only 4,400 words.

POPULAR PRESIDENT Indonesian President Susilo Bambang Yudhoyono was re-elected with nearly 74 million votes cast for him in 2009—the most votes ever received by a democratically elected official anywhere in the world.

FINGER FUNERAL

The Dani tribe from the island of New Guinea had an unusual method of mourning their dead relatives. It was customary for females to have one or two fingers chopped off at the first joint when a family member died, eventually leaving some with only shortened stumps. Observers have reported that a tribal elder would numb the arm by knocking the elbow, and then remove the digits with one blow of a stone axe. The finger-cutting ritual has been banned, but you can still see older Dani women bearing the results of the practice.

ICELANDIC FESTIVAL The town of Gimli in Manitoba, Canada, holds an annual festival that celebrates all things Icelandic. Since 1890, the Icelandic Festival of Manitoba—or Islendingadagurinn—has been crowning a Fjallkona (maid of the mountain) and reenacting Viking warfare tactics.

NATIONAL PERFUME Lithuania has launched its own national perfume—a blend of sandalwood, cedar, and musk designed to convey the Indo-European origins of the Lithuanian language as well as strength of character. Samples of the perfume were sent to Lithuanian embassies, hotels, and airports and to the country's soldiers deployed in Afghanistan.

UNDERGROUND HOSPITAL Ukraine's Solotvyno salt mine has a subterranean hospital ward for convalescing asthmatics and people with other respiratory problems. Its salty air is said to have created a unique microclimate that helps people who suffer from breathing difficulties.

HIDDEN TUNNELS In May 2010, police searched the residence of a man in East Austin, Texas, and discovered he had dug a three-story network of tunnels beneath his home. The tunnels went as far as 35 ft (11 m) deep and in several places were big enough to allow an adult to stand up.

LONGEST REIGN The 76th Maharana of Udaipur, India, is part of the longest ruling dynasty in the world. His family has ruled there since AD 566—that's an unbroken run of nearly 1,450 years.

SACRED RATS

At the Karni Mata Temple in Deshnoke, India, rats are treated with such reverence it is deemed a great blessing to have a rat run across your feet, or to taste food or water that a rat has also tasted. The 20,000 (and rising) temple rodents are protected, regularly fed, and if anybody accidentally kills one, they are expected to buy a gold or silver rat to replace it.

CLOSED WINDOWS To ensure that the exterior of Buckingham Palace, the home of Queen Elizabeth II in London, England, maintains a unified appearance, none of the front windows are ever opened.

NO DOORS The homes in the village of Siala in Orissa, India, have no doors. Residents believe a goddess watches over their village and protects it from theft.

WRAP FANS The last Monday in January in the United States is Bubble Wrap Appreciation Day, when bubble wrap fans celebrate the packing material, which was originally designed in 1957 as insulated wallpaper, by popping plastic all over the country. The day, known as BWAD, was started in 2001 by two radio DJs in Bloomington, Indiana, to fill the news void between Martin Luther King Day and the Super Bowl.

WAR TOURS A Swiss travel agency offers vacations in the world's most dangerous war zones. Babel Travel's catalog has package tours for Iraq, Sudan, and Somalia, as well as giving tourists the chance to spend Christmas in Afghanistan or enjoy a New Year's party in Iran. A 45-day vacation in Afghanistan costs more than $30,000—and that's without adding in the cost of travel insurance.

WHISTLING LANGUAGE The whistling language of Silbo Gomero has only four vowels and four consonants, and its speakers can easily converse while standing 2 mi (3 km) apart. It is used only by inhabitants of La Gomera in the Canary Islands and is communicated by whistling at different tones.

LOST COPY During its 40th anniversary of independence from Britain, the island nation of Fiji announced that it had lost its copy of the 1970 Independence Order, which granted the country self-rule.

Tree branches, metal skewers, and needles are just some of the implements used for piercing at Phuket's Vegetarian Festival.

CHAIN WHIPPING The Festival of Ashura is celebrated by some Shia Muslims with flagellation ceremonies where participants cut their own scalp with knives or whip their chest and back with chains.

FREE FLAGS Flags that fly over the Canadian Parliament's Peace Tower are free to residents who request one—but there is a 27-year waiting list to receive one.

STATUES STOLEN The Dutch city of Nijmegen removed ten large bronze statues from the streets in November 2010 after four of them had been ripped from their foundations, probably stolen to be sold as scrap metal.

SILVER LADY The Silver Queen, a 19th-century hotel in Virginia City, Nevada, has a 15-ft-tall (4.6-m) painting of a lady in an evening gown adorned with 3,261 real silver coins. Her belt is made from 28 gold coins and her choker and bracelets are made from dimes.

TREE HOUSE Farmer Xiong Yuhu from Xingping, Hunan Province, China, has built a house—with a kitchen, bathroom, bedroom, and lounge—at the top of a 50-ft-high (15-m) tree. Inspired by the Bird's Nest Olympic Stadium in Beijing, this luxury tree house is reached by a long wooden staircase. The structure is so solid that 18 adults have stood in the house together.

GETTING THE NEEDLE

At the Phuket Vegetarian Festival in Thailand, devotees self-mutilate by piercing their face and body with dozens of needles. Ritual vegetarianism in Phuket dates back to the early 19th century and participants at the nine-day festival perform acts of body piercing to purge others of evil spirits and bring good luck to the community.

REDNECK EVENTS

- ARMPIT SERENADE
- CIGARETTE FLIP
- BOBBIN' FOR PIGS' FEET
- MUD PIT BELLY FLOP
- WATERMELON SEED SPITTING
- HUBCAP HURLING
- BUG ZAPPING BY SPITBALL
- TOILET SEAT THROWING (REDNECK HORSESHOES)
- BIG HAIR CONTEST
- DUMPSTER DIVING

MUD-PIT BELLY FLOP
Another competitor makes a splash and gets down and dirty in the mud pit belly flop—for many people the blue riband event of the Redneck Games. Self-proclaimed redneck grandma Barbara Bailey has won the special event on several occasions.

BOBBIN' FOR PIGS' FEET
Caitlin Craft plunges face first into a trough of water and uses her mouth to grab a frozen pig's trotter during the 2010 bobbin' for pigs' feet contest. Whoever retrieves the most feet in the allotted time wins the coveted beer-can trophy.

TORCH BEARER
Proudly carrying the beer-can torch, Elbow, the official mascot of the Redneck Games, prepares to light the ceremonial grill to get proceedings underway.

ARMPIT SERENADE
2009 armpit serenader Aubrey Matthews delights the crowds by performing his winning song. Youngsters excel at this event as excess armpit flesh is not considered conducive to rattling out a good tune.

TOILET SEAT THROWING
A medal-winning contestant in the toilet seat throwing contest (redneck horseshoes) hurls away.

When people joked that the 1996 Atlanta Olympics would be staged by a bunch of rednecks, local radio station manager Mac Davis decided to reinforce the stereotype by organizing an alternative Redneck Games in East Dublin, Georgia. About 500 people were expected to attend; instead 5,000 showed up. The Summer Redneck Games was up and running... and hurling... and spitting.

Since then, the one-day Games has grown into a major annual event, showcasing such traditional redneck pastimes as hubcap hurling, watermelon seed spitting, and throwing redneck horseshoes (or toilet seats as they are better known). Rules must be strictly obeyed. For example, in the watermelon seed spitting contest, denture wearers must abide by the judge's decision if their teeth go farther than the seed.

One of the most creative events is the armpit serenade, where competitors cup their hands under their armpits to make farting noises or tunes. In 1998, one participant pumped out the entire theme tune to *Green Acres*, and in 2000 a 12-year-old boy moved spectators to tears with his armpit rendition of *Dixie*.

Many athletes return year after year, including Rawni and Rob Sprague, who got married at the Redneck Games in 2008. Dressed all in white, the bride and groom celebrated by performing the mud-pit belly flop, with friends of Rawni holding her train as she took the plunge. Now the couple renew their vows each year by being the first to dive into the mud.

Like their Olympic counterparts, there is no financial reward for the event winners—just a trophy. In this case, the trophy is a half-crushed, empty, mounted beer can.

Redneck Games

BIRD BRAINED

Sally Arnold from Kendal, England, returned home one day to find a perfect imprint of an owl on her window. The bird had flown into the window and left behind the eerie image—complete with eyes, beak, and feathers—before flying off. The silhouette was made by the bird's powder down, a substance that protects its growing feathers.

🅡 PANTS CARGO A man was arrested at Miami International Airport as he tried to board a flight for Brazil—with seven exotic snakes and three tortoises stuffed down his pants.

🅡 HIGH FIRE Germany's Paris Gun, a World War I artillery cannon, could bombard the French capital from 70 mi (112 km) away and could be fired so high that the rotation of the Earth affected its trajectory.

🅡 GLADIATOR FIGHT In August 2011, undercover police officers in Rome, Italy, dressed up as gladiators—complete with togas and capes—to prevent the escalation of a turf war between Italian gladiator impersonators who prey on tourists outside the Colosseum and other city landmarks. When the officers impersonating gladiators came under attack from the regular gladiator impersonators, they were rescued by other undercover officers dressed as garbage collectors and tourists!

🅡 SPEED CHASE Female police officers in Chengdu, China, patrol the city's Tianfu Square on rollerblades so that they can pursue criminals at speed—giving chase at speeds of up to 25 mph (40 km/h).

THE FEET ON THE STATUE OF LIBERTY ARE 25 FT (7.6 M) LONG AND WOULD REQUIRE U.S. WOMEN'S SIZE 879 SHOES.

🅡 TALBOT SOCIETY The Talbot Society holds gatherings for people named Talbot. They drive to Port Talbot, South Wales, in their Talbot cars, stopping en route at hotels and inns called the Talbot.

🅡 CLASS OF THEIR OWN A 2011–12 freshman class at Maine South High School, Park Ridge, Illinois, contained 16 sets of twins and three sets of triplets.

🅡 BLUES BROTHER Bill Smith-Eccles (aka Jake Blues) of Derbyshire, England, is such a fan of the 1980 cult movie *The Blues Brothers* that he wears sunglasses all the time—even on his driver's license photo, making him the only person in the U.K. that has been allowed to do so.

🅡 OUT WITH A BANG Following his death in 2009, the ashes of Alfonse Kennedy Goss, a keen member of New Zealand's Wellington Cannon Society, were fired from a cannon over the city harbor.

ALIEN CLOUD

Is it an alien spaceship hovering in the sky, about to land on Earth? No, it's a spectacular example of a lenticular cloud (*Altocumulus lenticularis*), a cloud that gets its name from its smooth, lenslike shape. When the wind on the sheltered side of mountains forms standing waves of air, and moisture in the air condenses at the top of those waves, it creates lenticular clouds. If the wind is constant, the clouds can remain stationary in the sky for long periods, leading to them sometimes being mistaken for flying saucers.

Leap of Faith

At the annual Goat Jump Festival in the village of Manganeses de la Polvorosa in northern Spain, a goat is thrown from the 50-ft-high (15-m) church bell tower and safely caught by villagers holding a large tarpaulin. The festival is based on a local legend about a priest who owned a special goat, whose milk helped him to administer to the poor. One day the hapless goat wandered into the church belfry and jumped off the ledge in fright when the bells rang for Sunday mass. The goat was luckily caught in a blanket and saved.

PICTURE THIS!

A driver was so preoccupied with getting out of the car to take a picture of the rooftops in Alassio, Italy, that she forgot to put on the handbrake... leaving the vehicle to roll down a hill and plunge through the roof of a house in the street below. The front end of the car ended up wedged in a bathtub, which fortunately was unoccupied at the time.

HARD LUCK

Making a sudden U-turn in an attempt to get out of heavy traffic, a driver in Houston, Texas, found herself in a lane of freshly laid cement. Stuck fast, she had no choice but to sit there in her $70,000 Lexus, while she waited for help.

HANGING AROUND

A New York Department of Sanitation salt-spreading truck dangles precariously over the road below after crashing through a wall on the second floor of a repair shop in Queens. The driver had to be rescued by a fire crew's cherry picker.

BUMPY RIDE

Following a wrongly positioned sign to the parking lot in a shopping mall in Liuzhou, China, Xiang Zhen drove her car down a staircase, where it became stuck. As startled shoppers fled, Xiang abandoned her car halfway down the stairs and phoned a tow-truck company to winch it back up to the street.

MIND THE GAP

Driving at night along a country road in Arnsberg, Germany, this motorist failed to spot that the road ahead had collapsed. Her car fell headlong into the gap, but she escaped unhurt.

DRIVEN CRAZY!

WATER RIDE

In Monterey, California, the driver of this BMW sports car escaped serious injury after accidentally propelling the vehicle off the edge of a parking lot, over a sun deck, and through a fence, before flipping into the swimming pool below. It's thought that the driver pressed the accelerator by mistake. Fortunately, the sun deck and the pool were empty at the time, and the driver escaped with only minor injuries.

MEXICO STONE

This house in Mascota, Mexico, is entirely covered in rocks! The house, which is also a museum, was decorated with rocks of different sizes by the owner after his wife passed away. They are everywhere, even on the picture frames, the television, and flower pots!

Rock Face

Photographer Peter Bardsley of Cumbria, England, spotted this creepy face formed by the reflection of a cave in the Hodge Close Quarry, in the Lake District. The skull cave (best seen when the picture is turned through 90 degrees, see right) can be seen only by abseiling 100 ft (30 m) down an unstable cliff, or wading through a 260-ft (80-m) mine tunnel. The quarry has not been used for decades, and its flooded tunnels and caves are popular with divers.

EARTH ON EARTH There is a place on Earth called Earth—in Lamb County, Texas—with a population of around 1,000. Founded in 1924, it was originally named Fairlawn until it emerged the following year that there was already a town in Texas with that name. The postmaster chose Earth as the new name supposedly because a sandstorm was blowing when he had to fill out a form for the postal authorities in Washington, D.C.

TURN, TURN, TURN Rongorongo—a system of writing in Easter Island—consists of about 120 symbols (including birds, fish, plants, and gods) and is read by turning the text 180 degrees at the end of each line.

SPEED MESSAGE To encourage drivers to slow down on country roads, the Australian town of Speed (population 45) renamed itself Speedkills for the month of March 2011. For the campaign, local sheep farmer Phil Down even agreed to change his name to Phil Slow Down.

SEA BRIDGE Opened in June 2011, China's Qingdao Haiwan Bridge, which spans the waters of Jiaozhou Bay, is 26.4 miles (42.2 km) long—approximately the length of a marathon. The bridge, which carries an average of 30,000 cars every day, is supported by more than 5,000 pillars. It was built using enough steel to build 65 Eiffel Towers, and enough concrete to fill 3,800 Olympic-sized swimming pools. More than 10,000 workers helped with its construction.

 Index

ACKNOWLEDGMENTS

Front cover (t) Nigel Hewitt-Cooper, (b) Bruce Lewis; **4** AFP/Getty Images; **6–7** Courtesy of Lockheed Martin; **8** (t) Amos Chapple/Rex Features, (b) Reuters; **9** Vyacheslav Oseledko/AFP/Getty Images; **10** (t) Imagine China, (b) © Chris Hellier/Corbis; **11** Reuters/Romeo Ranoco; **12** (b) Bruce Lewis, (t) Nancy Sathre-Vogel/Family on Bikes; **13** Nancy Sathre-Vogel/Family on Bikes, (c) © Anton Balazh/Fotolia. com; **14** (t) © Europics, (b) www.sell-my-photo.co.uk; **15** Fernando Bustamante/AP/Press Association Images; **16–17** Richard Grange/ Barcroft India; **18** Nigel Hewitt-Cooper; **19** (t) ChinaFotoPress/Photocome/Press Association Images, (b) Quirky China News/Rex Features; **20** (l) Karin Strandås; **20–21** (sp) Dominik Schwarz; **21** (t/l) © Bettmann/Corbis, (t/c) Karin Strandås, (t/r) © Julie Dermansky/Corbis, (b/l) Jean-Claude Francolon/Gamma-Rapho via Getty Images, (b/r) Rex Features; **22** seawhisper/yaymicro.com; **23** Mister Jo; **26** (t/l, t/r, b/l) Stephen Morton/Getty Images, (b/r) Richard Ellis/Getty Images; **27** AFP/Getty Images; **28** (t) Picture courtesy of Duane and Sally Arnold, (b) Magrath/Folsom/Science Photo Library; **29** Reuters/Desmond Boylan; **30** (t) © Europics, (b/l) SWNS.com, (b/r) Anthony Delmundo/Polaris/eyevine; **31** (t) Quirky China News/Rex Features, (c) UPPA/Photoshot, (b) KPA/Zuma/Rex Features; **32** Dee Allen; **33** Peter Bardsley/Fotolibra; **Back cover** Nancy Sathre-Vogel/Family on Bikes

Key: t = top, b = bottom, c = center, l = left, r = right, sp = single page, dp = double page

All other photos are from Ripley Entertainment Inc.
Every attempt has been made to acknowledge correctly and contact copyright holders and we apologize in advance for any unintentional errors or omissions, which will be corrected in future editions.